THE POET'S NOVEL

as a Form of Defiance: Indeterminate Frame

kin press

text by
LAYNIE BROWNE

artwork by
NOAH SATERSTROM

Kin Press
P.O. Box 682
Higganum, CT 06441
kinpress.org

©2020 by Laynie Browne and Noah Saterstrom

"A Woman, Thirty" from Can't and Won't: Stories by Lydia Davis. ©2014 by Lydia Davis. Reprinted with permission of Farrar, Straus and Giroux.

Editors: Meg Cowen and J.C. Mlozanowski

Cover design by Meg Cowen
Interior design by J.C. Mlozanowski

Cover image by Noah Saterstrom

ISBN: 978-0-9989293-2-3

THE POET'S NOVEL

I'm going to begin with a very, very short prose piece by Lydia Davis, from her latest collection, *Can't & Won't*. It's titled "A Woman, Thirty."

A woman, thirty, does not want to leave her childhood home.

Why should I leave home? These are my parents. They love me. Why should I go marry some man who will argue and shout at me?

Still, the woman likes to undress in front of the window. She wishes some man would at least look at her.

This story *could* be called a poet's novel. Poetry *could* be the woman in the window, single, free, while the novel is firmly married. The poet is like the woman who asks, why should I be married? Poetry, indeterminacy, loves me. This is ironic because poetry is a wild parent, providing more mutability than stability. Poetry may certainly argue. Yell. Does poetry love the poet?

Poetry is a window which enables belonging.

Does the unread text exist? Is it loved? Poetry loves the unseen text, the ignored text, the text which does not belong, the text which cannot decide, the text hidden.

And yet poetry also wishes to be seen. Why should I, says any poet, bind myself to a novel? A novel is imposing. A novel requires fidelity. How many novelists write more than one novel at once? Life beyond the page provides restrictions. Writing is an erotic act, a space in which more is permissible. Still, the solidity of the novel, from my vantage, as a poet, is daunting, less polyvalent. A novel suggests possession. In poetry there is abundant white space, more room for excursions, more emptiness to populate, more perfect omissions to imagine. Most poets aren't responsible for narrative in the same sense as novelists.

Or maybe poets understand narrativity as a different animal.

So the woman, thirty, or poet of indefinite age (poets being immortal) undresses in front of a window. It isn't necessarily a woman or a man wanting to be looked at. Imagine the scenario as you wish. The operative words here are "person," "indeterminate" and "freedom." This is the poet's novel, a poet toying with the idea of amorous attachment to unhinged form. A poet sets out to do it the only way a poet can, which turns out to be a myriad of ways, all of them intently distinct from the conventions of the conventional novel as we know them.

The poet's novel is a window where the conventions of narrative prose meet the open text of the poem. I refer to the open text, as described by Lyn Hejinian in her essay "The Rejection of Closure":

> "We can say that a 'closed text' is one in which all the elements of the work are directed toward a single reading of it. Each element confirms that reading and delivers the text from any lurking ambiguity. In the 'open text,' meanwhile, all the elements of the work are maximally excited; here it is because ideas and things exceed (without deserting) argument that they have taken into the dimension of the work."

The poet's novel solves the problem inherent in committing to writing any single book of prose, as an open text contains the possibility of many.

Back to Lydia Davis, "these are my parents. They love me." One way to shed light upon the poet's novel is to ask of any poet novelist, who are their literary parents? What tools and conventions have they tossed out the window along with fidelity to form?

And who might be lurking in a window across the way or in the street?

In other words, for whom does the poet-novelist write? What are the reasons a poet comes to the novel? One reason is simply to say, I am able to pay attention long enough. Another is to say, I'll never do that again! A third is to talk with other novels. A fourth is take up residence in the sentence, in the paragraph, in commodious mode. To build a house of prose.

Since I am in love with impossibility, I know I cannot address all of these questions, so I'll begin with my own convoluted path—and try to describe how I fell in love with this ill-behaving form—if it can be said to be a form at all.

But first, I promised to explain how I would dare to call Lydia Davis' gem of a story a novel. I want to see how far I can go, not to argue about form, but to overhear the arguments such a statement may elicit. Consider the statement: any text is a novel if the author, or reader, calls it a novel. Not particularly satisfying, but still, plausible as an entry, a poet's way to steal, or talk about intentionality.

Davis's short works could be called poetry, are categorized most commonly as "short fiction" and at the same time they gesture toward the poet's novel. How long must a novel be?

Can a handful of words encompass a novel?

More to the point would be a question: how short can a novel be? Are there edges, boundaries, limits to the form? If so, who is able to break them and how?

Gertrude Stein writes: "The only thing that is different from one time to another is what is seen and what is seen depends upon how everybody is doing everything."

So I ask now, how is everybody doing everything?

Many novels fail to provide the depth in acuity found in the shortest works by Davis.

Consider Virginia Woolf's lament in her essay on Modern Fiction:

> "The form of fiction most in vogue more often misses than secures the thing we seek . . . the essential thing, has moved off, or on, and refuses to be contained any longer in such ill-fitting vestments as we provide. Nevertheless, we go on perseveringly, conscientiously, constructing our two and thirty chapters . . . The writer seems constrained . . . by some powerful and unscrupulous tyrant who has him in thrall, to provide a plot, to provide comedy, tragedy, love interest, and an air of probability

embalming the whole so impeccable that if all his figures were to come to life they would find themselves dressed down to the last button of their coats in the fashion of the hour. The tyrant is obeyed; the novel is done to a turn. But sometimes . . . we suspect a momentary doubt, a spasm of rebellion, as the pages fill themselves in the customary way. Is life like this? Must novels be like this?"

The poet's novel says, no, life is not like this, poetry is not, and the poet's novel certainly will not be dressed. More likely undressed, as the woman in the window. Instead, the poet's novel often aligns with Woolf's assertion that:

> "Life is not a series of gig lamps symmetrically arranged; life is a luminous halo, a semi-transparent envelope surrounding us from the beginning of consciousness to the end."

And

> "There is no limit. . . —no 'method,' no experiment, even of the wildest—is forbidden. . . 'The proper stuff of fiction' does not exist."

When asked at a reading[1] about divisions between poetry and prose, and between short fiction and the novel in her own work, Davis replied, "I don't label ahead" (meaning she does not decide before she begins to write what genre she is creating), and noted that she thinks of her work as a "continuum," indicating that these boundaries between genres and forms are for her somewhat fluid, and not something she considers while she is writing. She said, "the material determines the length." When she was asked why she writes "short fiction" she invoked the Scottish poet Edwin Morgan and his homage to Zukofsky, the point being that the title of his poem, "Homage to Zukofsky" is three words and the poem itself is only one word, "the."

In Stein we find "A sentence which is in one word is talkative." And "A paragraph without words."

---

[1] In reference to Davis's reading at Bryn Mawr College, in April 2013. My imperfect quotations are from notes taken at the event.

What does this tell us about predetermined length of any form?

Davis also noted that while working on her translation of Proust she spent long days toiling over the Proustian sentence, so in her own work at the time she "reacted against it" and "decided to see how short" her works could be and "still have them have substance."

Understatement is one of her gifts. You could also argue, back to the woman at the window who loves her potential stalkers (or audience), that Proust is a source. As is Stein, for the poet novelist.

Proust, one of the most beloved writers to poets, has written a poet's novel. One of my definitions of the poet's novel is simply put, novels which are indispensable to poets, and novels which behave somewhat like poems. It may be useful to note, on this question—what is a novel and what is not—that even Proust did not know. A show at the Morgan Library & Museum[2] in New York City celebrated the 1913 publication of the first of the seven volumes of Swan's Way. Here one could see some of Proust's original handwritten manuscripts and notebooks, some of which have never left Paris. In one notebook, considering his book in progress he writes: "Should it be a novel, a philosophical essay, am I a novelist?"

---

[2] Exhibition at The Morgan Library & Museum, "Marcel Proust and Swann's Way: 100th Anniversary," 2013.

Back to the question, how I fell in love with this disorderly, erratic form. One of the first poet's novels I fell for was H.D.'s *HERmione*.

> *People ought to think before they call a place Sylvania.*

This sentence from H.D.'s *HERmione* stays with me. Her prose twirls, as Her Gart, her "heroine" is lost in a landscape she desperately tries to discern. Her "Oread" is here before considering the sea. Her Gart twirls in search of herself. What makes this a "poet's novel" beyond the fact that it was written by a poet? She wrote her way out, outside the thirty-two chapters, outside the liriodendron, which held her, outside the notion of properly buttoned. H.D. knew, the proper way to miss one's train was perched high in a tree. The proper way to be educated is to remove a fixed gaze out a window until it cracks, to leave, to quit. Hers is the story of liquidity, unfixity. Too many gazes. She became the woman at the window saying to herself, not, why should I leave, but how might I urgently depart? This is H.D. before she calls herself anything beyond "Her." She writes, "I am Hermione Gart, a failure." She had left Bryn Mawr and returned to a home which no longer fit. She writes about her relationships with George Lowndes (Ezra Pound) and Fayne Rabb (Frances Gregg). Essentially it is a book about unknowing, written in a style clearly in conversation with her verse forms. The book was written in 1927, about a time in her life perfectly unformed, which became stunningly formative. It is a book about deciding not to be possessed—by Pound, by parents, by an education which could not compete with poetry.

She writes: "People don't want to marry me. People want to marry me. I don't want to marry people." "One has to do something." A reader is amply housed within her revolving, spare language. If a sentence could speak back, hers would clearly say, "go."

H.D.'s imagist prose strips sentences bare. Short clipped phrases collide in parataxis and require the reader to wade—to take the spare and concrete text and re-imagine it through a series of repetitions.

Each reiteration becomes a new vantage which affords multiple readings enfolded within individual words.

"People ought to think before they call a place Sylvania, Pennsylvania. I am part of Sylvania. Trees. Trees. Trees. Dogwood, liriodendron with its green yellow tulip blossoms. Trees are in people. People are in trees. Pennsylvania."

Repetition disavows interpretation as singular. Her character is in motion. Enfolded meanings revealed in repetition suggest process over pronouncement. Observer—human—becomes organic matter, tree. Human, wanderer, whirler, becomes planted, rooted.

What happens when we repeat a word to the point that it becomes strange? Sylvania is inside Pennsylvania, tresses of trees. Treason. To depart from familial trees. Sylvania. Sylvan. Animus inside trunk, inhabiting liminal space, reveals more than we see. I found myself standing, by chance at Hermione's window. She was ensconced within a tree and behind plate glass, but in her thoughts, she roved.

How might a poet come to create a space as capacious as the novel, and yet as potentially destabilizing as a poem?

Where do the borders of the poem bleed into the novel? On the poet's novel, Bhanu Kapil writes:

> ". . . the lyric and textural scope of a novel-shaped space. The zone of impossible life. And how, in that zone, the poet might: stop time. And perform. Or install. Something." [3]

When I think of Kapil's *Incubation: A Space for Monsters*, I think of the form of the list, and how Kapil has transplanted this form so common to poetry into the form of the novel. A list is motion, instruction, a written choreography. We think through lists, live them, annotate and move through time non-sequentially as we insert our prerogatives. With each iteration on a list, as we enact it, who do we become? *Incubation: A Space for Monsters* is a book akin to movement as a form of identity. Laloo, a character, is in transit via hitchhiking, therefore having no idea which direction she and her window will move. Her body is spliced, part "monster," part "baby," part "cyborg," part "dream." She is moving in the direction of female identity, between borders, between safety and risk, between any fixed notion of intimacy and the question—how to be a person intact? She is revealed to herself within a moving

---

[3] "A Conversation with Bhanu Kapil"
jacket2.org/commentary/conversation-bhanu-kapil

landscape, but she is also hidden. She attempts to grasp convolutions and distortions of meaning that shake her to alertness. This book behaves as a poet's novel in that the interior movement within language and character is mostly intractable. We don't care where, literally, a character moves. *Who* she becomes *if* she survives is the central question, but this is not an answerable question. In a conventional novel, readers expect to be told—what happens to Laloo? Is she a reliable source of her story? Who is she in any one moment, and how can we trace who she has become by the end of the novel? A progression is demanded. Has she moved forward or backward? Are her movements intelligent? What is intelligence?

Readers of poet's novels want our relation to the text to be released from the expected conventions of telling. We want instead, to be shown one of any manner of ways in which a text can behave. We require, not a text behaving for an industry, but a text which wants to know something that cannot be told. An impossibility. A text that pushes against the painted sky one often arrives at within a novel—in horror.

"The line is a sentence but also a hand." [4]

---
[4] Kapil, Bhanu, Incubation: A Space for Monsters, 40. New York: Leon Works, 2006.

We require characters to laugh as they cut through the imaginary backdrop to address frame, perspective and movement, and to probe the interior or ulterior motives of any descriptive surface.

Inertia and cutting are required: akin to stillness or violence, both with similar, though wildly different, potencies. For example, "Hitchhiking, you tolerate the gun edging up your skirt or pointed to your head," "A monster is always itinerant," "Laloo, get out of the car now." "Divorce then re-marry the road at least twice." A setting is never static and a setting is never merely a setting. This could be said of action within any novel, but in a poet's novel action is not more important than stasis, arc is not the same as plot, character is not necessarily person, and time is often an operative device.

When I first arrived in New York City, in my early twenties,

I associated the novel with a never-ending series of rooms ...

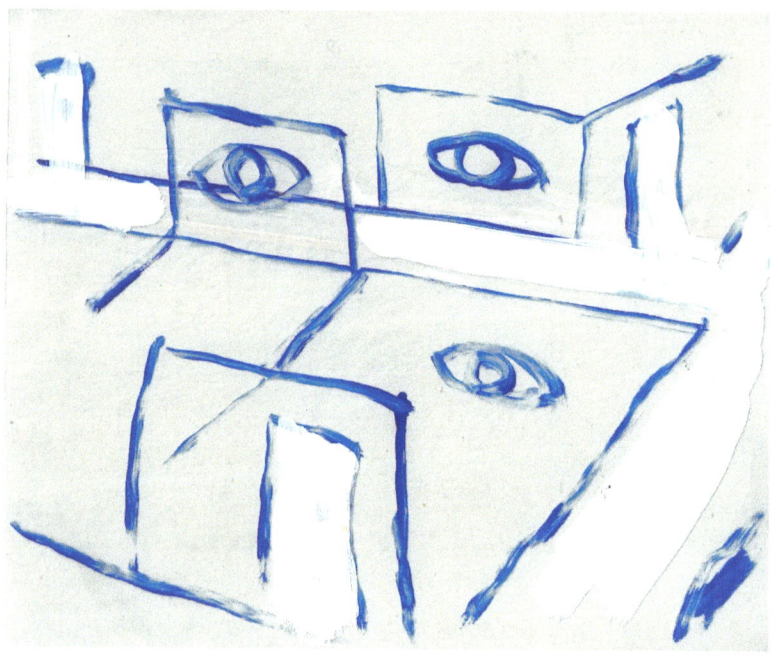

in contrast to poetry, and the studio apartment I shared.

But this was also a lie. The novels I loved might have no rooms. If the task of the writer is to create a habitable dwelling for the reader, then poets created lean-to's and structures of air. This is all wrong. Yet I include these thoughts to offer the mythos of the novel that I brought with me to the page. Poetry was electric. Poetry I could read at night and become more and more awake. Prose enabled sleep. To open a novel was to enter one's apartment, hang up a coat, kick off shoes and lie down with only the company of characters. This is known as reading.

Reading poetry was another beast or another way of wrestling.

Reading poetry was walking out into an unknown corridor in search of one's beloved, wearing a coat and nothing beneath.

You are very hungry and have not slept for a week. With care the text will feed you. You carry collage supplies in one hand, cooking implements in another, with one's third and fourth hands, several stacks of books, garbage, debris, homeless inhabitants, strangers, disembodied voices, dying landscapes, news feeds. Take this entire series of scattered images and arrange them in the palm of your hand. This was reading poetry. You could recite, but at the same time you took it apart. Maybe that's just how a poet reads poetry. I expect a reformulation of sense through a process rarely immediate. I never expect to be on solid ground or within reliable gravity.

Alice Notley writes, in an interview, "Poetry tends to abolish time and present experience as dense and compressed. Prose is society's enabler, it collaborates with it in its linearity. A poem sends you back into itself repeatedly, a story leads you on." [5]

In prose I always thought I could promenade, walk, distinctly in a line from one location to another.

Until I discovered poet's prose, or prose which behaved as poetry.

---

[5] "A Conversation with Alice Notley on The Poet's Novel" jacket2.org/commentary/conversation-alice-notley-poets-novel

Poets were always writing in this vein but the work was mostly ignored.

When I began asking poets about writing on poet's novels, for an anthology I am editing, a common response was: The poet's novel? Does such a thing exist?

In the 2014 Leslie Scalapino Memorial Lecture in Innovative Poetics, poet Simone White writes:

> "If I know anything, it is that I am working in a tradition of searching for ways of writing and an accompanying critical practice, a practice that never leaves questions of audience alone."

In her talk, she considers audience, identity, and literary communities and affiliations. When I read her words, I also connect them to questions of form which cannot be separated from questions of audience, any more than questions of content are separate from form. Form may be the first discernable invitation to a text. Form dictates where we find it. Form informs audience. White's questions about searching for ways of writing which do not leave questions of audience alone speak to a *now* inseparable from daily news, borders, identities, cities, bodies, technologies, and predicaments of ignorance, exclusion and erosion.

This tradition White describes of never leaving
audience alone, takes me back

to the woman, or the person in the window,
who might be tired of certain enclosures ...

wary of imagined others, but still seriously, and sometimes comically or tragically, asking how to write while remaining in that indeterminate space, inviting a future form to be born. The moment in the window is a precarious moment which keeps recurring for any living writer.

Interlude:

On impossible novels not yet written. Please write them. Write your own impossible novels:

One: Strategy:

I was at the grocery store with my list on one side, on the other side of a scrap of recycled paper, a scrawled forgotten poem. So in the store, looking at the wrong side of the paper, I found myself wondering where I might find, upon the shelves in front of me:

a colonial jellyfish.

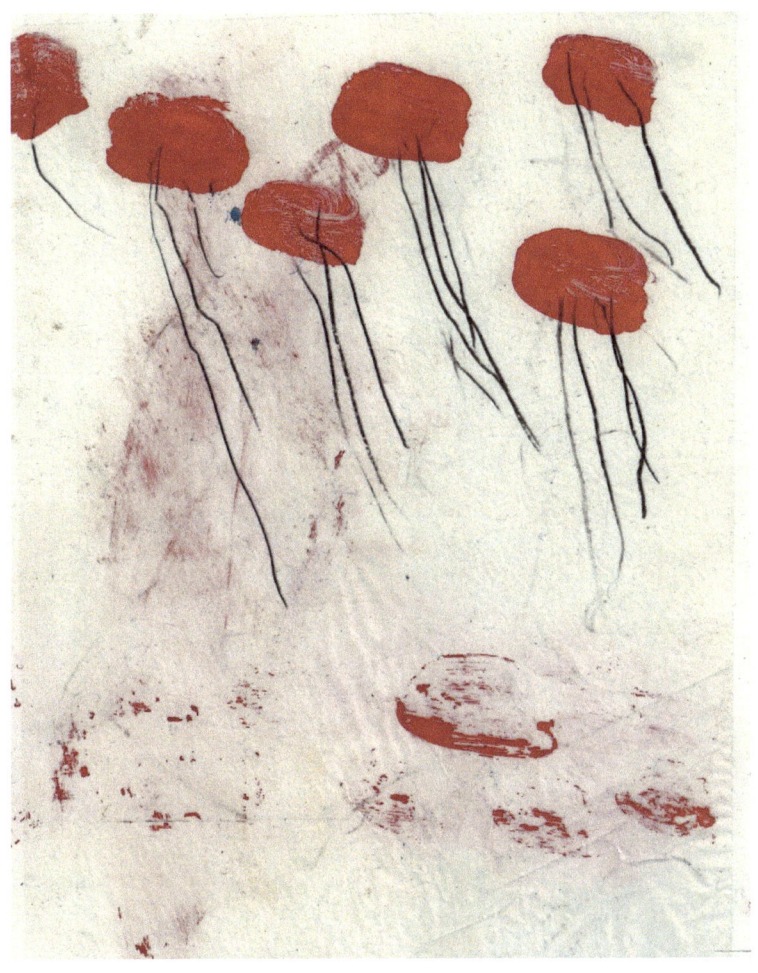

Process:

A person with a grocery list composed of lines of poetry. Could that be a novel? A novel approach?

Poets assemble your lists, your necessary supplies, colonial jellyfish. Reassign yourselves to look for what may not be found in that which already surrounds you. This is the Poet's Novel, your unseen resources, your ingredients forged. Write your sources and forms into being.

Simone White: "What project or affiliation am I being asked to participate in?"

Lyn Hejinian: "My writings have almost never taken form as single, independent entities."

Is it possible to separate genres? Forms? Actions? Texts? I'm less interested in separating than tracing a line of words along a page, to see where it will go.

I begin with audacious statements I don't yet know if I believe. So I have to find out, via writing, what I think of the form. If such a form exists. I am compelled to keep the company of texts which defy categorization. In the impulse of defiance. Is defiance a form? Or: instruction: intent: collect the roads of defiance. A new novel, which may be traveled by hand.

Any form that remains alive is mutable. Readable but not capturable, unregulated excursions. What is the point at which one animal becomes another?

A short piece by artist/poet Cecilia Vicuña, "Speaking to the Signs," precisely articulates the impulse I am trying to follow, as it shifts in and out of view, molts mid-page, punctures assumptions:

> "My mother recounts the day she found me 'writing.' No one had taught me how to write. 'What are you doing mijita?' she asked. 'I'm painting,' I told her, and went on speaking to the signs."

*One question of any writer is:
How do we direct our gaze?*

This brings us back to White's insistence on questions of audience. Lydia Davis's woman undressing in front of the window requires this question. Where is the gaze of the woman in the story? Behind or through closed doors. Closed eyes. Gaze out the window, gaze into the window from other windows, from the street. We are asked to question audience. A future or unwritten audience. What is a utopian audience? The poet's novelist may refuse to choose, and may choose looking itself, perception, as subject.

Brazilian novelist Clarice Lispector, writes of the "untellable instant, larger than the event itself." If a feeling is both "immaterial" and "objective" its seeming to "happen outside your body" only complicates an already many-tiered experiential reading or receiving process. The "untellable"—like a body in a novel unmoving, yet redolent with thought.

"The proper stuff of fiction does not exist." That does not make the poet's novel improper, but one could say that a certain courting of the improper comes into play when one is standing, considering where to direct one's gaze. Who gets to decide? In the poet's novel, sometimes we can hear the thoughts of the poet/novelist or a fictional voice, or an object, carefully considering. How close shall I stand to the window? How slowly can this happen? Or how quickly? Do chapters exist as days or hours? Poet novelists invent new methods of timekeeping, obliterate false affiliations, ask: what is indeterminate accuracy, in a written form now?

Amina Cain writes in her book *Creature:*

> "I am the reflection of someone who is dying. When I am looked at, it's not me that's seen. I am a giant mirror. You are too. See that woman lying down in the road? When you are in front of her, she is reflected in your eyes.
>
> To become a giant mirror, to stand in the middle of the wind knowing that's all you are."

The poet novelist knows something about reflective surfaces, dissolves into a giant mirror. And into the project of the collected, uninhabited, uninhibited and resourceful "I."

In Cain's book, the poet's novel is synonymous with finding the next step in a highly relatable but seemingly unsolvable problem. To clasp the next moment beside you, as it becomes translated into text, is all about attention which allows discovery, not fixity. We rarely consider sleep without reclining, yet we often attempt prose, within a poet's novel, in ways just as implausible.

What happens to the body of text when we shift, or lose consciousness, deliberately, while in transit? Maybe *lose* is not the correct word. Transpose. Transport. Translate. Deliberately misplace.

The mirror is where you don't see the author.

The author is not the woman at the window, but the situation of an author, or fictive construction, or the conglomeration of all the persons one could create.

The poet's novel is a refusal and a figure standing in a non-determinate place, toying with questions of genre, unloosing, undressing, cross-dressing notions of form, mixing, removing the skin from anything predetermined.

Karl Ove Knausgaard writes at the end of his six-volume epic, *My Struggle*, "I'm so happy that I'm no longer an author." He feels entrapped by the only vehicle which allowed him to escape the facades of fiction. Himself. He calls this a literary suicide. In no longer using himself as material, he thinks he will be liberated. He argues hopefully, in an interview, that perhaps this will allow him to live with more presence, and less distance from his life.

This question of the livable distance between life and the novel is relevant to the poet's novel. Sometimes poets turn to fiction because they have material they can't approach any other way. With this question of distance in mind, I'd like to finish this talk with my own wrestling with the form of the poet's novel—as a writer of poems and novels.

Outside the window:

Looking for self-knowledge, I began to throw myself off every page.

I was no longer good at knowing things. My thoughts threw themselves over every bridge.

This has nothing to do with suicide. Everything to do with death. The death of the world of forms as I knew them. I inherited the taboo of first person and so abandoned "I."

In the end you have to turn. Walk. Stand. Swim. Page as bridge or window.

The world still turns its back on. Ecstatic experience.

I thought I wrote a novel once in a dream is only a sentence. I've been alive with this assumption for a while now. It isn't really much power. I'm climbing out of it. I threw myself off of every edge, every page, searching for what it means.

What is a self in fiction? One vehicle of the poem is dissolution of person.

Time is an element turning pages in a poet's novel. How concisely can you turn person to icon, or the reverse—icon to permanent memory—lapse in the middle of a road. Steep curve.

The writer throws herself out every window, crawls under each utterance and listens to the underside. A poet's novel is the underside, the window, and the possibility of throwing oneself out a window. Or from a balcony. While listening to ecstatic music, thinking one could almost fly. No one was harmed in the making of this metaphor. What I'm talking about is risk, and abandon. Impetus to find what is ahead, and desperation that comes from seeking out forms, alive, not yet born, fluent, and willing to leap. The woman cannot stand in the window forever. One book ends. Another begins. At some point you turn, move, exit.

Once I didn't have such thoughts about windows. A window was merely a place to pine or a place to gauge the weather, the larger world beyond the room in which any words were written, unwritten. The world was a place to try on novels which might be happening in any of the windows above.

I knew that however many windows I considered, however many pages I threw myself from, I was still the mirror in the street, the dissolution of a person. But what is a person? I wanted to be a character, but failed. Each day I awoke and found myself still a person with severe biases, and my own beloved persons who could appear as characters, but who I knew were always persons in disguise and could not be written. How to embrace them? How to escape them? Fiction provides such windows.

But fiction still wanted me to lace and dress the thirty-two chapters. I refused.

I flung myself from the page and looked to poets who borrowed structures. My main object was to write a book which was a spiritual memoir, not using myself as material. My main goal was withholding, and also understanding, for myself, certain happenings. The only way for me to find out what had happened was to write the novel.

At the time I was living in Arizona, in the same community as House of Representatives member Gabrielle Giffords, who was shot outside a grocery store in my own neighborhood. Gabrielle Giffords, who attended the same synagogue as I did, and suddenly Arizona was on the map again, and not just for bad legislation. At the time two persons I loved were dying. At the time the Occupy movement was just beginning. What could I do to consider difficult questions about violence, illness and loss, not using my own experience as material. But using the moment, which appeared relevant, the now, yet unborn. I wasn't the only one in tears.

I turned to fiction. And I turned to chemistry. I conceived of a novel, *Periodic Companions*.

I coaxed the elements of the periodic table into characters...

based their relationships upon chemistry and asked what would happen when they tried to answer questions about non-violent protest using chemical signaling in human tears. Tears for senseless acts of violence which surround us. Emotional tears contain chemical signals which lower testosterone.

What if we could cry upon command? Imagine, an entire airport, school, city or occupied war zone— filled with people crying upon command, ending the impulse to violence. Writing this text enabled me to imagine a redemptive function for tears.

Form also helped me to answer the question: why poets can be so indeterminate. We are made of mercurial impulses. I wanted to find the unwritten narrative about non-violent protest in which tears invented their own story. It was not my story. Narrative had to be inside the materiality of language, not using language as tangential or a means to an end. I wanted to collaborate with language. To let the letters and the elements have their way. I hoped to witness this happening each day as I sat to write, my eye disappearing, dissolving, and a text appearing word by word.

A poet with novels inscribed upon her sleeves knows, a novel is also a concentrated gaze.

The gaze of the poet novelist is refracted into the imagined gaze of each reader, each passer on the street, each moment of dissolution, refusing to be settled or known. You meet the poet's novel at a party and can get nothing out of her, still she may be the most compelling collection of assertions you've never met. Part person, part animal, part mirror, part street, part assemblage, and obviously, prevarication.

You know when you've met the poet's novel because at that moment you also have flung yourself into the arms of defiance.

This text was originally written as a talk for Poet's House in November of 2014. Thank you, Stephen Motika. Special thanks to Cecilia Vicuña for performing with me. In 2015, I presented a version at a seminar at Université de Paris 8 Vincennes Saint Denis. Thank you, Vincent Broqua and Brigitte Felix. In 2016, yet another version at University of Washington, Bothell at Convergence. Thank you to Jeanne Hueving. Tremendous thanks to collaborator Noah Saterstrom. Thank you to all the poets and novelists who have made this piece possible. Thank you to Meg Cowen and J.C. Mlozanowski for bringing this book into being. Excerpts from this talk originally appeared in a series of commentaries written for *Jacket2* on the Poet's Novel in 2013 (jacket2.org/commentary/poets-novel).

Sources

Amina Cain, *Creature* (St. Louis: Dorothy, A Publishing Project, 2013), 101.

Lydia Davis, "A Woman, Thirty" in *Can't & Won't : Stories* (New York: Farrar, Straus and Giroux, 2014), 62.

H.D., *HERmione* (New York: New Directions, 1981), 4-5.

Lyn Hejinian, "The Rejection of Closure" in *The Language of Inquiry* (Berkeley: University of California Press, 2000), 42-43.

Bhanu Kapil, *Incubation: A Space for Monsters* (New York: Leon Works, 2006), 3, 72.

Karl Ove Knausgaard, *My Struggle, Book 6* (Brooklyn: Archipelago Books, 2011).

Clarice Lispector, *Água Viva*, trans. Stefan Tobler (New York: New Directions, 2012), 4.

Edwin Morgan, "Homage to Zukofsky" (Scottish Poetry Library), www.spl.org.uk/poetry/poems/nine-oneword-poems.

Marcel Proust, "Marcel Proust and Swann's Way: 100th Anniversary" (New York: Exhibition at the Morgan Library & Museum, 2013), www.themorgan.org/exhibitions/marcel-proust-and-swanns-way-100th-anniversary.

Gertrude Stein, "Composition as Explanation" in *A Stein Reader*, ed. Ulla E. Dydo (Evanston, Illinois: Northwestern University Press, 1993), 497.

Gertrude Stein, "More Grammar for A Sentence" in *A Stein Reader*, ed. Ulla E. Dydo (Evanston, Illinois: Northwestern University Press, 1993), 550.

Cecilia Vicuña, "Speaking to the Signs" in *Spit Temple* (Brooklyn: Ugly Duckling Presse, 2012), 41.

Simone White, "Leslie Scalapino Memorial Lecture in Innovative Poetics" (2014), media.sas.upenn.edu/pennsound/authors/Scalapino/SPT-Lectures/Simone-White-Leslie-Scalapino-Memorial-Lecture-in-21st-Century-Poetics.pdf.

Virginia Woolf, "Modern Fiction" in *The Common Reader* (San Diego: Harcourt, 1925), 150-154.

Laynie Browne is the author of thirteen collections of poems and three novels. Recent books include: *In Garments Worn by Lindens*, *Periodic Companions*, and *The Book of Moments*. Her poetry has been translated into French, Spanish, Chinese and Catalan. She co-edited the anthology *I'll Drown My Book: Conceptual Writing by Women* (Les Figues Press, 2013) and edited the anthology *A Forest on Many Stems: The Poet's Novel* (Nightboat Books, 2020). Honors and awards include a Pew Fellowship (2014), the National Poetry Series Award (2007) for her collection *The Scented Fox*, and the Contemporary Poetry Series Award (2005) for her collection *Drawing of a Swan Before Memory*. Recent collaborations include a public art project, "Dawn Chorus," a curated constellation of poetry in thirteen languages by twenty-eight writers engraved in The Rail Park in Philadelphia with visual artist Brent Wahl. She teaches at University of Pennsylvania and at Swarthmore College.

Noah Saterstrom was raised in Mississippi and educated at Scotland's Glasgow School of Art. His paintings reside in public and private collections in the US and abroad. He has collaborated with writers including Laynie Browne, Anne Waldman, Joan Fiset, and Kate Bernheimer. He has published art-related essays and articles and was a regular contributor to Nashville Arts Magazine. His painting "Road to Shubuta" was acquired by the Mississippi Museum of Art in 2018 and his painting "Maeve" is the cover of Ann Patchett's newest book, *The Dutch House* (Harper Collins, 2019).

www.ingramcontent.com/pod-product-compliance
Lightning Source LLC
Chambersburg PA
CBHW041508010526
44118CB00006B/191